T0208910

Songs of the Beloved

ELIZABETH SPANTON

BALBOA.
PRESS
A DIVISION OF HAY HOUSE

Balboa Press books may be ordered through booksellers or by contacting:

Balboa Press
A Division of Hay House
1663 Liberty Drive
Bloomington, IN 47403
www.balboapress.com
1 (877) 407-4847

Because of the dynamic nature of the Internet, any web addresses or links contained in this book may have changed since publication and may no longer be valid. The views expressed in this work are solely those of the author and do not necessarily reflect the views of the publisher, and the publisher hereby disclaims any responsibility for them.

The author of this book does not dispense medical advice or prescribe the use of any technique as a form of treatment for physical, emotional, or medical problems without the advice of a physician, either directly or indirectly. The intent of the author is only to offer information of a general nature to help you in your quest for emotional and spiritual well-being. In the event you use any of the information in this book for yourself, which is your constitutional right, the author and the publisher assume no responsibility for your actions.

Any people depicted in stock imagery provided by Getty Images are models, and such images are being used for illustrative purposes only.
Certain stock imagery © Getty Images.

Print information available on the last page.

ISBN: 978-1-9822-0407-5 (sc)
ISBN: 978-1-9822-0408-2 (hc)
ISBN: 978-1-9822-0409-9 (e)

Library of Congress Control Number: 2018905604

Balboa Press rev. date: 05/09/2018

Dedicated to John Roger, John Morton,
Mystical Travelers in the Movement of Spiritual Inner Awareness.

CONTENTS

Gems Of The Beloved

"LOVERS OF GOD"

Under the tower clock of love
In the time of souls:
Discontinuous, irreducible to the computation
Of day, month, year, calendar-
Two Encountered.

In words of indefinable fluidity
The intellect stimulates Wisdom of the other.
The relationship measured only against God relationship-
Separation, reunion annihilated.
The discovery: divine freedom in the other.

One instills vision and language in the Other-
The rendering of Spirit as Word.

Loving, she hears the sound of the falcon's drum.
A sweet wind wafting from the Friend's garden blows,
Imparting fragrance of Jasmine.
She delights in this Lion of God.
Her condition transcending yearning, desires.
Quitting place and entering the Placeless,

Love consummates the Essence.
Intoxicated, she dances Indestructible Union.

"BE MICHELANGELO TO ME"

Sculpt away till the angel in me appears.
This block waits to be worked on.
You can see where the chips need to fall.
I leave all to your design.
I'll not resist the pain
Of loosing those parts of me that
Deny your Majestic Manifestation.
You alone know the Divine Form inside.
No longer do I control.
With angel wings, I would fly home,
Die from bliss known by that part of me not chiseled
Centered in the Oneness, present in the All.
Silence me; let the chiseling begin.

This marble block is given.

THIS VOYAGE FROM SELF TO GOD SELF"

This voyage from self to God Self
This covenant with Love:
Be Joseph, surrender to the well.
Be Moses, lie to the pleasures of Egypt.
Be Jesus, emit Light of Transfiguration.
Be Da Vinci, access creative imagination.
Be Rumi, come from the heart.
Be Francis, sing a joyful Canticle of Oneness.
Be Michelangelo, expose prejudice.
Be Blake, see Infinity in a grain of sand.
Take the walk of a dragon through this world of darkness,
Bringing magical miracles of mystical love from your cave.
Take the lion's stride.
Be a voice as huge as a bell ringing silently.
Use the leopard's grace and speed,
On this voyage, this Promised Covenant,
From self to God Self.

"LIGHT GIVING LAMP"

There's a king in the house performing servant-hood,
Praying out of love, and when he says,
"God is greater." he leaves this dream world.
He knows how to not make his existence his companion.
Severity is not his, only the world of gentleness.
He has placed that great dome of the ego behind him.
His gaze does not see faults, he has no complaints.
His freely-choosing quickly goes to the Real.
He takes sovereignty over his own
Soul, state, attributes, speech, his own silence.
He has taken on the light of His Majesty.
He, a mine; he is gold,
A light giving lamp, a worthy companion.

"BEYOND TIME"

The deepest part of me listening
With an ear empty while being full hearing
"Die, let go, be given, surrender all,
Let nothing be left in your Cave, earth dragon.
Beloved is waiting for a permanent residence full of Light.
Practice the silent Zen shot of bow and arrow.
Listen to Tibetan bowls humming.
Hear crystals poised silently on rock shelf speaking, "Be Still!"
Embrace that in him to which nothing can cling.
Give your heart to this.
Empty of forms, all forms are contained in it.
Only Love and the lover can resurrect."

"Secret Sound"

Unspeakable Name,
Essence of everything,
Silent sound thundering through All
Speaks Itself, creating universes,
More of Itself.
I listen in quiet silence
Listen to your love song
For I am singing You
Within the within of Your
Unspeakable Name.
In me expressed-
A Word
For you to speak Your Love.

"GOD WORDS"

As gold is tried in the furnace,
Let dragon's love flames burn
Bring forth the immortal "HU" vibration
In human words.
Let silence reign
Until love song,
God's love letter,
Be spoken.

"MYSTICAL DRAGON"

Sh…let Silence speak
I am a transcendent, mystical dragon.
I thought I was a lamb.
The breeze of eternal spring dances under my wings.
Feeding on intention, I am strong.
I am the sound of "HU"
Singing love songs all over the world.
Enticing all to enter the silent cave—God's workshop
Where all trace of work and profession is lost
In Nothingness,
So the hidden one, the person of God,
May shine forth from inside
In all its glory.

"The Alchemist"

God's Hu-The Alchemist
Has set ablaze the dry leaves of my human knowledge.
It is wind crushing my every emotional life experience.
As my lover, the Divine Hu
Has completely ruined me. I don't care.
Under the ruin is treasure, a cure.
A smile with the generosity, the grace of God.
It has set me alive to God's sweet love
Opening me through emptiness-
For everything else
Has lost its meaning, its fortune.
Because the smile opened me to the beautiful one inside of me,
To the Light under the cloak.
Now, I flow like a dancing stream toward the Beloved
Rushing toward the Beautiful One.
Now, Love before me, behind me
I am lost to Love.
Love-the seeker, the goal, the seeking itself.
The Alchemist-God's Hu.

"REQUEST"

Man of Spirit, whisper to me Divine Mysteries.
Inspire me with the sweet sound of the flute
Crying out like a lover
That tells of separation.
You have refashioned me to the Divine Image.
Taught me from the religion of Love
Given me the vision to see the reflection of the Divine Other.
Bridge us to the Sublime
That wants to be known in the world
That He might be adored.
Let us live knowers of God!
I, a fool for God,
Abandoned to the Love of God.
By way of feeling, I move my intellect
Toward gnosis-an order of encounter
Not lower as some would claim.
Rather, an initiation as a mode of perception.
God manifested that He might adore and love Himself.

"GOD'S DELIGHT"

I fall into your laughter, fun,
Feeling God's Delight!
Your eyes, overflowing with sweetness,
Innocence and honesty,
Resonating a joy filled wisdom found also in me.
I don't see a man liable to decay
But to his spirit, eternal in its grace.
The body is a wintered world
We'll let Eternal Spring blossom with our Love.
In Your presence,
I paint pictures of Heaven Here on Earth,
Bring forth Eden once again.
You ask my intentions, I reply,
Constancy and friendship.
In return, you ask, "What do you want of me?"
I reply, "steadfastness in grace-filled love
From eternity.
That's how long I've loved you."

"LOVING THE DIVINE"

You are the pearl of a shoreless sea,
The precious jewel of an endless cave,
You are a boundless sky with a million moons
And a zillion shining suns.
You are the Wisdom born of supreme Truth.
You are a man of God well hidden, but
I find you in my heart-a priceless treasure.
The company of a Saint.
This earth path is not safe to travel alone.
I'll sit in the company of a Saint
Where love is life
And life is loving.

"'CHRIST-ED' FRIEND"

In my soul is a bride.
She breaks down my ascetic door.
The arrow of his eyes wounds me
What messages pass between his eyes and mine.
What can't be conceived nor understood
Enters when the bride worships him.
With his help, my loving gaze is fixed on eternity—
The time of union when time has no substance.
His essence fills my heart and soul
My youth returns, I am eternal.
He is drunk, without wine.
I drink the elixir of love.

"FRIEND"

You brighten my eyes.
The wine you offer takes me out of myself into the Self we share.
You carry gifts.
I see you- as you secretly are in silence-the Essence.
Like a bee I make honey from thoughts of you.
I am separated and yet in union with you.
You give a cup of pure fire to your closest friend.
I walk into your orchard, pick God-fruit.
You are the sun dissolving dull overcast.
You dress in the flower of God Qualities.
You are an invitation to walk with you.
God's secret lakes form in your bay.
Your being pulls me like a river out of the
town in me and onto the plain.
My only sadness is when I am not walking in step with your essence.
You are a walking fire. I am eaten by flame
and smoked out into the sky.
I get to change and disappear.
A swan waked to the land not governed by sadness, doubt,
Where fear of death is unknown.
You are Myself.
The bee of my heart dives into you.
You are the dawn, that awareness in the middle of the night.
You are fragrant wafts of fresh baked bread.
You are sunlight over the countryside.
Because of you, I am like a fish under water beginning to say words.
I am a prayer; you are the Amen.
Sing us into union wearing white pilgrim cloth.
I shake hands with an oak tree that is thee.
You are practical, immensely powerful and solid, open to service,
Silently living what is,

Non-assuming, humble, holding integrity.
Compassionate, given to God,
Faithful, passionate, reliable, moderate, servant,
Brilliant, creative, a lion-master of his own being,
Cherry blossoms of spring-intoxicatingly
beautiful pulling passion out of me,
Gold-brilliance.
Medicine, every word you say heals.
You are quiet, still, an indescribable message coming on the air.
God's lover,
Sweet beyond telling,
Servant to the ocean of God,
A sun within, warming all who meet you.
Seeing your face my concerns change as lake water rises into mist.
You-the morning shade.
Golden mind, perceptive, a free bird.
Your wind shivers my tree.
You make my dance daring enough to finish,
Wanting what I see in your heart.
My mouth taste sweet with your name on it.
The smile tells gentleness inside.
Friend, the Beloved.
A Lover of Chocolate.

"CHRIST-ED FRIENDS"

You invite me to remember that I am in a glorious Spirit City,
Not the Dream City full of good and evil that I am passing through.
You let me taste the true Friendship of God Love.
You lead me to my inner teacher
To listen to Spirit.
You help me see that form is just
The clothes of Spirit
You help me rest my lower appetite and
Feed on Wisdom.
You challenge me to lift
My pettiness, my lack of self-worth.
You expose me
To the Divine Me.
You teach me to ask forgiveness,
To open the
Eyes of my heart.
You crush my intellectual swimming,
Put me into the ark with Jesus.
You show me Light that is not of this earth,
Tell me, "Seek sanctuary in the Name."

In Return:

I would be faithful
Keep the Presence from being
Interrupted.
Be loud silence, listening.
Be contemplative joy,
Not an empty reed but sugarcane for you.
I was fire, but now I would be Light for you.
I would lead you to the Friend who gives

Fullness, without food,
Roses and wild flowers without spring,
Healing without medicine,
Instruction without books.

By my side, you would gather pearls by the bucket full.

"'CHRISTED' FORM BLOSSOMED ME"

I am a freshly opened lotus flower
In a pristine garden, this blessed morning.
His loving wakened me.
I hold the secret.

He joyed me forth to my full blooming.
See what love has made me.

Beautiful in my radiant form.

God saw Himself in me,

And smiled out my blossoming.

"Only Source Satisfies"

Denied the physical
I look deeper and deeper
Trusting this vinegar is honey,
Cut through the façade of this world-
The earth bears weight of every misery.

I leave the earth and all its hardships
Enter the Garden.

There is nothing but poetry and love songs now
How can sorrow enter my heart?

I am a true lover, not alone,
My heart is filled with the Ocean.
I listen to what my heart is telling me.
The smile of that angel lands in my heart.

I am like the stem of the flower
Quivering in the morning breeze
While the flute song plays in my heart.

"BEGGAR NO LONGER"

I sought down the labyrinthine paths of learning:
Scriptures, lectures, books.
Allowed the ascetic in me to blossom.
Followed the saint's paths, did charity,
Prayed to a God above me, outside myself.
Bowed, worshiped, adored.
Still, I remained the beggar
Till one day love appeared.
I lost myself.
Became Beloved.
Alive in my heart, mirrored Beloved.
He, the radiant beauty of a starry night.
Went to inner place.
My soul one with his soul.
God - love.
Found Gold Inside Me
No longer the beggar seeking!

"OPENED"

In illusion, there exists my time line.
Projecting energy into the future.
Emanating from me,
Rays from the Holy of Holies
I am light's beautiful lotus flower opened.
Consciousness clear as a crystal stream.
Incense rises.
The seal of Solomon has silenced all opinions.
The small moon knows its fullness.
Give the beautiful one a mirror.
Let me fall in love with myself
To kindle remembering in others and myself.
Still, in the Now, though the stream water may look clean,
There's unstirred matter on the bottom.
There's need to dig a side channel-drain the waste off.

Helpless, I turn to the Lord of my heart.
I am not a prophet, but I'll go the way of the prophets
Let them speak-
Be the ear
Listen to the teacher within
Become a school.

"ONENESS"

What metaphor will speak this oneness,
From this world of seeming separations?
This oneness found inside my heart
A world without dimensions
Expanding me eternally.
Wisdom within governs,
Leading me to tenderness, to kindness.
All I see is me, for I am Source.
There is no separation
Only opposites
Through an act of love
Opposites unite.
My only challenge is to be myself,
The "I Am".
The mind in me is the mind in all.
I am boundless,
Merged with God
In all dimensions
At all times.
I feel no pull to change anything
I only respond to needs.
Life flows on its own
In me, through me.
In this Oneness.

"LOVE GARDEN"

The flowers bloom forever
The birds sing an eternal song
The moment we enter the garden
You and I.
With clean heart and pure love
I would walk with you in the garden today.

We need no words, love is full,
Content in its simplicity and silence.
Within, the sound of "Hu" vibrates us as lovers of God.
We walk in harmony with birds, plants, waterfalls, each other,
Living and singing the Word made Flesh.

Coursing through us, one sweet, prolonged,
Eternal kiss of union joying our walk.
This day, heaven on earth in us.

"AWAKENED"

The Source is within me
This whole world is springing up from it.

I came here to experience
Becoming plant, then animal,
Finally human, endowed with Intellect, Will,
Knowledge and Love.

I was never made less by dying
I fear no death.
How perfect I have become.

Even my heavenly body will pass
As I plunge into the vast ocean of Consciousness.

I would become the Ocean
Forgetting the drop.

There is nothing to do here,
But to un-remember the story
Till I know only Me.

There is only to Be,
To dance in this Presence
To drink wine.

I would have, no tale left to tell,
Quiet body, listening heart.
I belong to my Beloved,
Without remembering, I remember.
The crow in me is the white dove now.

The desert of prickly cactus is flowering.
The rocks turn to precious jewels.
In the sight of my Beloved,
I rename the weary world.
Every note of my song
Longs to ring
With the sweetness of my Beloved's voice.
Every breath
Would be fragranced
In my Beloved's flower-wind.
I would serve joy instead of bread to my guest!

"UNITY"

Lovers seek unity
Master has made us so.
He has placed His Light in our world.
We, the ones drawn to this Light,
Shall end all other desires in winning this Light.
We lovers, willing to loose all-
Our very souls in God's love.
The only ones who can understand
The wisdom of Unity

"Hurricane Calmed"

Hurricane winds,
Wild with desires.
Fling me to my center, the calm.
My wanting's, my longings,
Ceasing in stillness.
My counsel:
Know
The Beloved's Presence
In the silence of your heart.
There, shower kisses that are
Without beginning or ending.

Take communion with his essence.
You, the flute, open to the
Beloved's flower fragranced breath,
Playing together the 'Christed' Love Song.

Know joy that reigns eternal,
Without end or beginning.

TO BE NEAR THE KING"

Moving from the world of duality to unity
I return from the vestibule to the sanctuary,
the high seat of the soul.
Like a bird, I fly to my natural home
Wings outspread, cage open.
To be near the king, like a falcon, I let go of the kill.
Grace-wind lifts me.

"THE FACE OF GOD"

Every door is open wide:
The door of the palace, the chamber of the Beloved's.
Still, I sometimes seek like the mouse for its tiny hole.
Till I wisely fill my soul with so much love,
And run toward the saints.
I turn my night of sleep
Into divine revelation.
Hold the Grace of God
Behold the Face of God
Become its home
Forget my thoughts
Follow my destiny,
Become the Christ.

Unbind, dear heart,
Remove the locks,
Be the Key.
The Christ.

"One Desire"

On fire with holy desire-
Father, Mother God,
Create in me divine cooperation, each moment.
From many selves, one voice,
One action
Your one desire.
From You are born the power and life
To be this Song, your will desired.
Renew in me this song.
You are my intention.
I AM Christ Consciousness
Knowing and claiming that I Am God Manifested
I am the living Divine Will.
I live from the deepest part of myself
From my whole heart, from my greatest
Passion, courage, and audacity.
My whole animal energy and life force is used
To flood my entire grasping mind with Love.
All of God's perfect Kingdom is mine.
All of love is mine.
All who love are mine,
For I know nothing but Love

"BE NOT UNAWARE"

Be not the drunk man in the city, unawake, unaware.
Paradise in Eden, my responsibility!
Mountains could not take the load, man can.
He it is whose thoughts create the elementals
Who either shapes devastating storms or gentle rains of blessings.
Man's thought, word, action, feeling,
Each is taken care of, is raised, brought to fruition,
Remains and pursues its course for it is life.
Each never dies.
Man who breathes Spirit's Breath into Being must ask
What am I creating today?
What am I not creating today?
Inner doing is most powerful
Every moment Brahman Creator, Creates.
Man is always doing.
He is greater than any king.
He is Being,
Whose thoughts are great, Deep - higher than brain.
From being, man creates.
Come, Love,
Create Paradise once again on Earth.

"WANTING ONLY GOD"

I would be a clean piece of paper untouched by writing
That the pen of God thoughts might ennoble me.

I would be silence listening
That I might hear flutter of angel wings.

I would build my fortress of the Presence
That I might leap into God protection.
I would be empty, fertile earth, where nothing is growing
That heaven might sow thought seeds that yield love action.

I would see expansion in contraction
That I might look as a sage to the end.

I would be without desire
That I might live in God Harvest.

"Sweet With the Infinite"

Once a scholar loving books
Living from the marks of a pen.
I now follow footprints of a person
Whose presence teaches more than all books.
I long for a meeting with the Friend, with Majesty,
Who lives on Light.
My pilgrim heart with its spiritual emptiness waits
To be filled with light, illumination
That I might know myself as light.
I am like a grape vine
That needs intimate companionship, with ground
To open into earth's darkness
Become selfless,
In the presence of my origin.
Discover once again what I really am.
My lips have become sweet with the infinite.

"THIS MOMENT"

I awake with winged heart.
Like an eagle high, alone
I fly across the sun
Toward my ship,
Toward the ocean.

Eagerly, with great readiness
With full sails
I cast off into the vast sea,
Where winding rivers of longing have returned me.

I join them to be the boundless drop
In this boundless ocean
Of consciousness,
Bringing with me
My tenderness, my longing heart,
Made sweet by loving all the beautiful, the good,
The unloving
To that dwelling place of our greatest desires

The heart of God.

"BELOVED ONE"

Most High Beloved,
You are what we want,
What we do.
You are everything!
Keep us looking high, seeing Light
Lest we identify with our shadow.
Dissolve earth's two worlds into one.
Make us so drunk with love
That we dance free, in ecstasy.
Let us belong to the strong hearted
Who walk narrow and thorny paths,
Where colorful flowers and blue birds singing
Are found amidst howling wolves.
Let us sing not to still the fear
But to celebrate the laughing, Living Joy.
God invited us to a loving feast,
Not to a graveyard funeral.

"LOVE LIVES HERE"

"Good bye" to life's myth:
We are in exile.
Here, the Kingdom.
Its secrets, hidden in the ordinary.
Consider homeless man
As he shields companion from cold winds.
With yesterday's newspapers.
Witness the tenderness of kisses
Placed upon the crying child.
Watch night stars sparkle brilliant light
Inspiring awe, wonder.
Love hides in the humblest places,
In cricket's song,
In the aroma of mother's kitchen.
Fields of sunflowers delight the soul
Radiating Loveliness.
Common words, "How Are You?"
Bond hearts, longing to touch.
Love sings in the Opera House, in the Tavern,
In the whisper of breeze touching trees.
Love bubbles forth in mountain streams,
In children's laughter.
Why seek heaven in another place?
Love lives here

"HU"

Airplane roaring above
Fountain gushing, splashing,
Children laughing, talking, playing,
Ice cream truck sending repetitive song-
Like popcorn popping in a space
Where one seeks meditation-

She silences all with free heart
Holding the noise
As God.
It's all God.

Soon the tone shouts the Name
Lost in the One Word.
"HU"

"COMPANIONS OF THE HEART"

What use is the head?
An animal lives through its head.

The secret heart cannot live through the head.
A HUman lives through his secret heart.

He has a spacious character and disposition.
Speaks broad and capacious words that open up the heart
He forgets the world and its narrowness.
He, a servant of God, knows the words and tongue of God.

He has come out of the dust of this existence
Where poverty is complete.
God can be seen in what you find.
You find God.

I seek companions of the heart.

"COMMITTED"

Committed to wakeful Conscious Love
Open to receive Conscious Love
Made for the Beloved.
Like the reed flute singing
For its dirt bed beginning,
My heart sings
For the experience of My Source
Through love experience
Devoted to learning through Friendship
I claim mental dominion.
I shape the love- bed
Soft, sweet, rose petals
Designed for God-Love unity.
I open to teacher, knowledge, discovery.
To live wakeful Conscious Love.

The experience of My Source.

"NAME OF GOD"

Longing to know love more deeply
I search while looking right at him
I fill my heart with his love
Let silence take me to the core of existence.
I know a sacred decree
Lovers must seek the Beloved,
For we are made to know our own soul.
I have placed my light in his heart.
He has placed his light in my heart.
The fire burns any veil
Don't be frightened to look
The Beloved is staring you right in the face.
If you have fallen in love,
That is proof enough.
The grief we cry out from
Draws us toward union.
This longing to be the Name of God
Empty of self and filled with God Love
Let us know union with the core of each other
Let us breathe the name "HU"
Be the Name of God.

"ONLY LOVE"

All is in God's heart
My substance, only love.
I am nothing and everything as I enter this moment of creation-
Letting, not wanting.
God, as itself, living with conscious Christ mind
As this human form.

Silence!

"RADIANT ONE"

Breeze of Eternal Spring dances inside us
Let the world in us feel and forget the sorrow.
No bitter medicine is needed to heal.
Savor, drink sweet water of love.

Then dance the Divine,
Long for a meeting with the Friend, with Majesty,
Who feeds on Light.
Move inside, let Love dance out
Be the Radiant One.

"UNITY"

Knowing who I am,
I'll build a home.

I'll live within God,
No longer within this body
No longer in self-importance, no keeping accounts,
No longer worrying, no judging behavior
I'll simply play my part on this stage of life-
An invisible guide
Like the scent of jasmine
That tells where the inner garden is
Where there is Eternal Spring.

What a human sees, he becomes
I'll see myself as God.

"LIFE GIVING DEATH"

Waiting, listening, alone in the sarcophagus,
I die to the lesser light
That I may rise to the Greater Light.

Holding the blossomed Lotus Staff
Disciple of Osiris
I kneel humbly before the altar
Asking to be clean of heart
That I might see God,
Be a lover of God,
Dedicated to the Service of God.

I receive the key
Unlock the Mystery of my life
-God's will-
The inner truth of God
An integral part of my being
Holding me with strength and purity
Till I am all Truth.
Radiant, Shining Light,
Birthed from Spirit,
Loving God, Myself, and You.

"GIVEN"

Name erased,
Given.
I live empty.
Filled with my Beloved's breath,
A flute playing for the dance.
Playing Living Music.

A love song-
Firing union.
Birthing Christ
Into the dance.

A new happiness befriends us
As we work at offering our lives.
Truly Given.

"CHOOSING LIGHT"

Teach me each moment Thy holy Love
That I might joy and be Your Living Love
Eating from the Tree of Life.
Knowing Union.
Make me radiant, energetic Soul Light.

Give warmth, creativity, insight
That I might walk each breath
As Christ .

Invisible, higher beings, assist
Keep me on vertical path
Consciously aware,
Living wisdom
Living Light

"LET ME BE SUN TODAY"

I would be warm sun on this earth day,
Where cold has frozen playful waters.
I would gently melt crystalized judgments.
I would coax the spring crocus flowers of goodness
To peek out from under the snow laden criticisms.
I would be like Spring's soft, sweet, warm flower-wind
Hugging all crying for hope, healing.
I would be like quiet burning coal,
Radiating gently, while listening to the story.
I would be warmth that smiles fears away.
Be like the soft feathers of a lark's breast
Mothering patiently, promise of tomorrow.

Let me be useful today as Your Sun.
Use Me
Your Living Love

"EDEN"

Transcendence finest hearing-
Hearing silenced "HU"
Laughing, sacred Word
All pervasive
Ever present wave
Singing out
Worlds without end.

Structuring harmony
Of the all in the All.

Transcendence finest seeing-
Seeing with God's eyes
Delighting in light creations,
Manifested beauty
Of the Singing Sun

Structuring harmony
Of the all in the All.

Transcendence finest
Touch, taste, smell
Encountering one Beloved.
All in harmony with the All

Mind's play of duality
Obliterated

Silence ever deepens, reigns

Intuitions inspire
Immeasurable Intimacy

Soul homed
Heaven's harmony here
Eden now on Earth

"DIVINE FRIENDSHIP"

As the fragrance of jasmine concedes to the
Vibration of the breeze,
Carrying it into the high firmament,
Two yield to Divine HU Wind.

Abolishing separateness, Divinities unite.
The beginning – A glance.
The ending – Eternity

It is as though some magic and strong gentleness
Restored both spirits to this life from another.
Rebirth of happiness in torn hearts.
A revolution of wings, once injured
Now soaring
Journeying home on
God Wind

"HONORING THE BELOVED"

We share a sacred decree-to seek the Beloved.
Let silence take us to the core of life
Let us be a dancing stream flowing toward the Beloved.
Caught in this body, we look for a sight of the soul,
I see your face glowing with light-
The inner splendor.
My soul kisses your feet, Beloved.
Incenses you with my Beloved's flower-wind
As we play this day in Heaven.

"DEDICATED TO THE SERVICE OF GOD"

I receive the key
Unlock the Mystery of my life
-God's will-
The inner truth of God
An integral part of my being
Holding me with strength and purity
Till I am all Truth.
Radiant Shining Light,
Birthed from Spirit,
Loving God, Myself, and You

"LETTING GO"

Spinning within Divine Play of Motion
Fling me to the Silence
That wakes me to Thee
Illumine my darkness
Fill light in my veins
In love's golden brilliance
Let joy be my fame.
Let me see the world playing
Let me know its embrace
Let me be in your love,
Honor this Place.

"DIVINE SMILE"

My thoughts remember:
I am Drunk with God,
Flow over with ecstasy,
Addicted to his Divine smile.
I taste the Sweetness of Sugarcane
I ride huge waves of blue ocean water
I see brilliant rainbows in misty sky
Divinity's smile, it's everywhere.
Namaste
"The God That Is Thee Within Me"
Divine Communion

"BIRD OF THE SEA"

Elizabeth: I am like the bird of the Sea
That was birthed on land.
I was born for the Ocean
I seek the Ocean.

God: *The roar of the sea is here*
Let go of earth's clay jug of perception,
It has such a narrow spout!
Listen with your heart.

Elizabeth: Then grace me with forgetfulness
Till I remember only Thee in this Now
For I am the furnace,
You the spark that fires Union
Bestow your Divine Smile
That I may know your ecstasy.
The joy of the Ocean

"BYZANTINE EARTH FORM"

Like a child in mother's womb,
I own two worlds.

Ineptly, I experience, dwell in darkness,
While yearning for light.
I feed on food that doesn't fill,
Hold death while holding life.
My breathes are numbered,
I drink waters that don't quench HUman thirst
My claiming knowing something,
Blocks Magi's secret Mysteries.

Similarly, in another world,
I am radiant Living Light.
Live eternal breathing,
Spirit's
Contraction, expansion.
I am healed without medicine.
Nourished without food.
Knowing nothing, I know the All.

"Modern Hurt"

By day,
Over the wide ocean,
Sea gulls soared on white wings.
By night,
A moon sailed through dark cloud rifts.
The man moaned like a bird unmated
His wife and another made holiday together.
Crying like the white doves in a church tower
He longed for lost love she wasted on urban pleasure.
Her infidelity so open.
His constancy poured out.
Inside, so empty.
The wind from the sea blew fiercely.
His world vanishing like foam on the waves.
He was rudderless, adrift.
I offered him my sands of goodness
Gave him my tattered heart.
Still, sharp sands pounded
On his open tender heart.

"BENEDICTION"

Joy hides in the humblest hedges this spring
It is imminent that it laughs and blushes green
Already patches of snow concede to bursting blades.
Mist of green stirs, caressing willow branches—

"Mirror"

Man contemplates
His own reality
The mirror becomes God

God Contemplates
The Names and Qualities
They, the Living mirror.

"SMILE"

Receiving love's sacred,
Serenely sweet smile,

Winter's shade is lost
To eternal summer.

His sovereign eyes
From heaven shine.
His golden shape
From eternal line

Divinity's presence
Caught in time

"FEET AND WINGS"

Humans on foot
Angels with wings-
In a taste of wine
That blocks understanding-
Longing for freedom from feet and wing
Living in beautiful forms
That We might talk and feel
And taste Your Glory!

"THE FRIEND"

Youth Spent
Pining long
King David's words:

"My soul is Thirsting for the Lord,
When shall I enter and see the Face of God?"

Sustained seeking-
Discovered now
As Love's Face
Uncovers Me.

Present in His Eyes
The Presence of the Christ
Divine Smile.

One with His Soul,
His radiant Face,
Smitten,
Heart burst
Pure Light.
I see Him now
He is my sight.
The Face of God.
The Christ.

"FLUTE SONG"

Beloved breathes the world through me
Forever new, forever young.
A love song sweet cannot be found
Any place, more kind, profound.
We dance the trees, the zephyr breeze.
We dance the stars, a twinkle far.
We dance the rainbow, church bell rings.
Our love expressed through flute breath sings.
The day, the night.
A reed song sung.
Inaudible,
Forever young.

"FLOWING SILENCE"

Flowing Silence,
You that led winter wind,
Your withering-
Now, wisteria flowers this springtime,
You blossom forth cascades of violet flowers.
Tomorrow, you flow again to seed.
Teach me patience
While I live this winter sleep.

"GIVEN FROM INSIDE"

Given from inside,
Jasmine flower wafts fragrance
Wisteria blushes purple,
Angel trumpets bursts forth from quiet buds,
Bird cracks through egg,
Nightingale serenades her love song.

Given from inside love expresses
This midnight morning
Truly wanting to be given.

"MY FRIEND"

You are the freshness
Of that which has never been born.
You are not a confusion of atoms,
You are clarity, a perfect design.
A shimmering diamond.
Your value cannot be measured
You are infinite Sun
Shining in the presence of the Presence.

"BELOVED"

Like a dancing stream
I flow toward the Beloved.
I search for Him looking everywhere
While looking right at Him.
Caught in this body
I look for a sight of my soul.
The petals of every flower brings a message
From the unseen world.
I keep looking to find Him.
Silence my looking.
Give me vision of the Presence.
Fill my heart with Love notes
Soak my every cell with the wine of Christ.
Let me vibrate living Love.
Kiss me over and over.
Be sweet wind passing over.
The fragrance of Love is my wish.
In the face of my beloved
In the smile of my beloved
All beauty is revealed.
One sight. That is my wish.
Let me be drunk on the Love
Found in His Heart.
I stop dancing in the stream,
Fix my gaze on eternity.
He is inside me waiting to be kissed.

My heart, Christ's heart, in Love's Sea,
Loving my Beloved eternally.

"ROCK DEITIES"

Windermere

Rock deities poised against misty skies
Majestic structures defying definition
Infinite shapes, designs
Blending in harmonious scene
Ancient yet new
Each form master crafted
By powerful ancient waters, winds, sands.
Standing content and given to the silence
Present in Eternal Now Action—.

A deep resonance
Fullness upon fullness

My heart moves, embracing Creative Intelligence
In this play field of all Possibilities.

"WINDERMERE"

Life abounds in this earthly heaven.
Birds drink from this rain rich land.
Bold bullfrog croaks.
Orange dragonfly flits from rush to rush.
Ladybug lands on my hand.
An ant stops, seeking direction for food source.
Pink water lilies blush from lily pads.
Baby goat bleats for mother from high rocks.
Fresh green moss hugs trees.
White sheep shed winter wool.

I listen with my heart,
Touched with wonder, awe
At God's Grandeur!

Shadows fall at sundown,
Announcing coming night.

I bow at the rock shrines encased in carved out rock.
My beloved walked on these grounds before me.
I wake to his presence in this exquisite, wonder world.
Moved to adoration,
I worship the Lord
Who guards this Eden.

"METAPHORS"

The Hidden One is my beacon
Yet his works stay invisible.
My soul scuds like a ship on a fair wind.
As I wing my way home,
I fly into my own heart.
I, the mine, where loveliness is quarried
Where I see Him.
Metaphors—my keys for traversing
The topography of my Soul

"MY FRIEND"

You are the freshness
Of that which has never been born.
You are perfect design, bell like clarity
Ringing with sharp simplicity,
God, only God, is heard.
Your value cannot be measured.
You are infinite Sun
Shining in the presence of the Presence.
It is eternal trysting time,
My dear Friend.

ONE WITH THE LIVING HEART

There is a passion in me
That does not long for the fleeting
Still, in an embrace, I held
The Essence without attributes
The key fit the lock.
Holding absolute purity,
I held one living in the Heart.

"BELOVED"

I am iron filings
Your love the magnet
My soul dissolves in you
With you it mingles.
Your love and I blending
Your affection and mine partners.
My heart is desolate without you
Oh Beloved, enter!

"BE LIKE"

The gold of my intelligence
Is scattered over little thoughts.
Be like Solomon,
Visit the Beloved early in the morning.
Gather all your separateness
Offer it up to the Spiritual Heart.
Only love can silence
The voraciously hungry mind
That separates and confuses
With many answers
Stop the constant traffic.
Love is the answer
Listen with the heart.

"CONQUERING DARKNESS"

This is my Father's world
And to my listening ear
God's melody of love rings clear.
I claim this world for my Father
The Christ, the Spirit
The Light of God flows.
The dark is conquered in me
I am heaven on earth
Aligned and at home in God.

"TEACHER"

What is my teacher but the beauty of the Beloved?

What book and lecture do I read but his Face?

The penetrating remembrance of the High Throne of the Friend

What lesson do I learn but that of astonishment,
enthusiasm, trembling—
Drowned in God and drunk on love.
With this man of heart, the rock that I am becomes a jewel.

"ETERNAL SPRING"

The Great Spring is ever here.
Its sweet fragranced air blows through my garden.
Caught in this needy, imperfect body,
I must sense with my soul.
The Great Imposter challenges my vision once again
With Winter Winds wanting in.
But still I am companion of that Ancient Lover.
Around the still point of ecstasy He whirls me.
I ask that every pour be filled with the wine of that Silence.
To once again see with the sight of my soul.
To drink the wine of that Silence,
That I stay drunk with his essence—
Live in the Joy of Eternal Spring.

"Man's Grandeur"

God is speaking man's grandeur.
He shouts out like the voice of a peacock
He breathes out in crescendo,
Like cymbals clapping, Tyco drums drumming.
Calling, "Wake Up!"

Why do men stay deft to His Voice?
Claim not his royal place,
His grand part in this royal play?

The beggar coat is worn;
Attuned to moaning, sorrow, pain,
Ears stay deft to Divine melodies' call,
"Come, Dance the Divine!"

Yet, for all this
The invitation stays open.
And though the sounds aren't heard today,
A celestial voice keeps singing—
Love's call-eternal:

"Come, Dance the Divine!"

"GOD IN MAN"

Like sea-wind sweeping through sandy shores
Till all is wind swept,
Man's heart breathes forgiveness till all is love swept.

Like a billion stars spinning through the night
Love's firecrackers light the darkness of life.

Wonder happens as man passes through harshest danger.
Though intricate and subtle, his powers reveal, expose
The God in him;

Ancient sleep,
Let go of us!
Be
Roaring waterfall
Waking this sleepy land body
That holds hurt, seems dark,
Harsh, maimed, ugly, irreparably damaged.
Waken us to Christ's body
Realized in joy.
Like flash of lightning,
Transformed
Radiant in His Light
Recognized as whole, as lovely-
in every part
The Beloved.

"Camping at Arrow Head"

Wild winds sing through majestic tree's pine needles
Raindrops pitter-patter as they dance on nylon tent.
I wonder in awe at the separate sounds singing in harmony.
Made one by listening heart
Unity in diversity.

"DESERVING"

Lifted up by wings of Love,
I ask,
"Father, forgive us.
Remove our tattered clothes of life.
Dress us in silk,
Befitting our Divinity."

"TRUSTING LOVE"

Wanting nothing,
I am constantly surprised.
Presents every moment,
Timed in perfect sequence.
Trusting love

"MAJESTIC TREES"

"Tall, stately, noble trees,
Speak, I am listening."
"Rise from this earthly plane
Reach up for the Heavens
Seek the highest first
While staying grounded to love's needs:
Nesting, protecting, nourishing earth's life forms.
Play
Remember me surfing high blue sky waves
In the roaring, wild wind.
Watch squirrels scampering with me in branches high.
Stay aligned to nature's laws,
That you grow strong and straight."
With open heart, I listen.

"SERENE SOLITARY SCENE"

Only silence knows
This Mountain taken by snow.
Sitting stately at night,
Glistening companion to moonlight.
Full moon shining
Casting shadows of pines.
So may my Light
Cast shadows of delight
In the silent stillness of to be,
God's silent Presence known in Me.

"ONLY SOUL SATISFIES"

I long for your sweetness to visit me.
Like humming bird, I am restless in body,
Not knowing where to find the nectar.

Like butterfly on leaf
-Wings folded-
I stop and rest in prayerful, silent trust,
Till once again as hummingbird,
I move deeper into this flower,
Love envelopes.

Tasting this sacred soul nectar,
Hummingbird bows with devotion
Consecrated by this flower,
Where All is One.

"CITIZEN OF HEAVEN AND ROME"

I hold Rome
-The life of the city never lets go-
Nor do I want it to go for
I would make every visible thing
Ennobled
By living Wisdom.
The chords of divine reverberations
Are expanding every form into
Total grandeur, a
Magnificent edifice made by
The Knower
Expressing Itself as
Word taking form
So It can be Known.
I expand,
Open Heaven in Rome

"MEMORIES"

On this autumn day, spring's Beauty lingers in my heart.
I loved it yesterday in Yokohama's Gardens,
Where cherry blossoms bloomed a prodigious benediction.
Memories, like drops of dew upon blades of grass,
Lift with morning sunshine.
Beauty sees, remembers that I loved her;
Transforms each dewdrop into cloud of raindrops.
Nourishing California's Gardens this springtime coming.

"YES"

"Yes," just "Yes" my heart says when you are near.
Every instant we shall tear a thousand veils.
See only the Beloved everywhere.
We look upon the world as invisible.
Doubt all that is visible.
Find the Love,
It's a game of hide and seek.
Like birds, we shall fly high as Lovers,
We shall look beyond our eye's range.
Encounter Highest Heaven waiting to be seen.
I see you there, you are breathing,
The one Breath,
That is breathing Me and Thee.
Love is doing Us
Love Itself

"DIVINE FRIEND"

I'm in on your secret.
Your golden light fills me.
We need not meet somewhere.
You're in on my secret.
I carry the secrets of the hillside,
And the songs of the forest.
I talk to the ears of your spirit.
We have long been in each other.
I thought I knew who I was,
But I was you.
The beauty of our friendship
Is eternity gazing at itself in a mirror.

"LOVE PLAYING"

This whole Earth
A great game of hide and seek
Being lost and being found.

Longing and fulfilling
Secrets and surprises
Expansion and contraction
Ignorance and revelation
Being everywhere and nowhere
In time and out of time

This whole Earth
Simply
Love playing.

"SEEING BEYOND"

Personality-what is that but illusion.
See no lack, no pain-look inside.

Mountains look small beside the grandeur.
The heart's love but a breath beside God-Wind Love.

I could sing forever,
Never would I begin to describe your Face,

Oh, Handsome One!
Having been denied the physical for now,
I have discovered your Secret.
I am drowning in this Love,
Wine-filled Ocean that is You-Hiding.
Surrendered to You-God Love
I see you everywhere
Loving Me in Thee,
Eternity gazing at Itself

"Yes" only "Yes" my heart says when you are near

"LET ME BE SUN TODAY"

I would be warm sun on this Earth Day,
Where cold has frozen playful waters.
I would gently melt crystalized judgments.
I would coax the spring crocus flowers of goodness
To peek out from under the snow laden earth.
I would be like spring's soft, sweet, warm flower-wind
Hugging all crying for hope, healing.
I would be like quiet burning coal,
Radiating gently,
While listening to the story.
I would be warmth that smiles fears away.
Be like the soft feathers of a lark's breast
Mothering patiently, promise of tomorrow.
Let me be useful today as Your Sun
Use Me
Your Living Love.

"BIRTHDAY POEM"

Humming bird's fluttering wings.
Nectar filled flower waiting, secretly given.
Light filled jewels radiate, designed for attracting only one
The one who knows of the Garden's Eternal Spring,
Who rests in that Inner Place
Where they sit together,
Her soul by his side.
The garden blooms forever
In the union of his heart to hers.
Full of Fire
She dances without music,
In Garden Breeze

"OWNING LOVE"

Without your presence, I am like winter
With your presence, I am like a rose in the habit of spring
Hold me in your heart as a Presence
Then I will be in your Presence, younger than springtime

"LONG AWAITED PERFECT FRIENDSHIP"

Given
I receive and experience His Heart
Aligned to me in Hu vibration
This lover of God loves me
Fills me
Awakens Divine Expansion
Friendship's boon:
Eternity Now

"Courting the Divine"

Two butterflies pass
Dancing a love song.
Winged strong from within
Drawn by mystery to each other.
Courting with each winged movement
So, let us court
Dancing the Divine.

"THE LOVER'S CIRCLE"

I look upon this world as invisible
To have entered the lover's circle.
From where this life breath comes
In that Presence, I am lost to this world.

"COMMUNION"

I have entered the heart of a man and shared Divine communion
He opened me to that part of me that sings spring's sweetness
Heaven visits, in this garden.

"CHOOSING THE NIGHTINGALE"

A parrot, talking for the taste of delicious fruit,
A falcon flying to find my royal place,
A peacock, seeking for praise through a thousand eyes,
Or shall I choose a nightingale singing
Being someone in love.
Who knows the intimacy of God,
A fire of passion burning in Spirit depth,
A constant touch of sweetness linking all hearts
In a rapt ether of eternal love,
This, I would be!

GEMS OF THE BELOVED

"LOOK WITH YOUR HEART"

If you care for a blessing,
Look with your heart.

I am a clam,
When I open my mouth for a drop of water
Discover the pearl.
Inside's living love
Waiting to be discovered

What? A lump of coal?
I am the clarity of a diamond of infinite worth.
If you care for a blessing,
Look with your heart.

PEACH RIPENING

I live inside Presence
Like a peach drinking in sunlight
Hurrying toward its own sweetness

"WISDOM"

Like sap silently creating white lotus
Like acorn designing mighty oak
Like seeds generating golden wheat fields
We pull our existence out of consciousness
We made this body, cell by cell.
The body developed out of us, not we from it.
We live in this world
A harp touched by love singing
Like bees making honeycomb
We make this body, cell by cell
The body of Christ.

"ONENESS"

Be one with the cave whose silence
Grows flawless rubies, sapphires diamonds.

Be one with clams
Whose discomfort designs exquisite pearls.

Be one with night
Whose darkness shines stars in splendor.

Be one with rich earth
Whose cradling brings forth mighty oak.

Be one with Solomon,
Who speaks loving wisdom.

Vanish into the All
You'll shine like the Sun.

Be nothing
You'll be everything.

"THE CARVER"

A carved piece of wood reveals there is a carver.
Strange phenomena
This human tribe
Attempts to hide
The majesty,
Infinity, the Carver.

"JAPANESE SCREEN"

A Japanese screen
Nothing on it
I hold for the Absolute
To reveal an idea
If a picture is to appear

"SHABDA"

Stirring Hum
Coming from unbounded emptiness
Emptiness filled with dynamic silence
Emptiness moving to know Itself
Its beauty
Its power
Its unconditional love.

Moving-creative hum
One Unbounded Ocean of knowingness,
Of consciousness in motion,
Fully awake within itself.
Knower, knowing itself as the Known in love's vibration,
The Process of Knowing.
Knower, Known, the Process of Knowing-
One becomes three while remaining unity.

Swirling hum, in virtual field,
Swirling tornado in motion
Its Vortex touching down to point
There – creation's manifestations:
Particles, waves of light
In the Unified Field.

In that Now
As Word
God can be heard

Every form, from man to stone holding voice
Discovered by ears open to hear.

Beauty of the heart
Grandeur of the earth
The echo of HU.

God's desire to know Itself—revealing.
God's desire to be Beauty –expressing.
God's desire to be Unconditional Love –loving.

The un-manifest, manifests.
Word heard,
Light seen,
Dancing in this gift called Life.

Man,
God-Word of consciousness,
Harmony of divine sound, light, forms.
A Knower.
Known
Through love's vibration,
The process of Knowing.
One becomes three while remaining unity.
Knower, Known, Process of Knowing.

"God- Word" humming.
God speaking
Song singing.
Light radiating.
Love, loving."

Hu-mans
God-Words
Each, tone and rhythm unique.
Singing revelations of
Dynamic silence,
Unbounded emptiness,
Eternal life.

Humming Voice of the spheres
Cosmic symphony
Calling Itself to Source

Hu
Love song of God
Hu
Heart of God
Hu
Calling,
Embracing us home.

"CHOICE"

I live in this Ocean of Consciousness,
Experiencing myself.

I swim lively above ocean waves
—No light
—No land anywhere
—Thick cloud cover
I fight to stay swimming.
I let go, fall to ocean floor silence
—Breathe "HU"
—Gather pearls
—Relax
Ocean caresses me,
I kiss back.

"LETTING GO"

Spinning within Divine Play of Motion
Fling me to the Silence
That wakens me to Thee
Illumine my darkness
Fill light in my veins
In love's golden brilliance
Let joy be my fame.
Let me see the world playing
Let me know its embrace
Let me be in your love,
Honor this Place

"SURRENDERED"

My all is given to the All.
My all is busy with the All.
Had I known the cost of this union-
I would have - not entered it so freely.
Had I known the cost of separation,
I would consecrate this union a zillion times.
How blissful,
Receiving zillions of kisses every moment!!

"GIVING"

He who gives coins for God's sake,
Will be given coins in return.
He who gives smiles for God's sake,
Will be given smiles in return.
The generosity of the God lover
Surrenders his soul,
Himself, to Love's commands.
He will be given back a true Friend
Who will always nourish his soul.
And with his soul always green
He will grow into a tall tree,
Flowering always with sweet, light fruit,
Whose growth is interior.
He will taste the savor of Life
And know the power hidden in serving.
He will be released from this world
Like a bird from its egg.

"DETACHMENT"

Joy springs forth when flesh is shackled.
It demands to be light and free.
It craves dance and play.
Bind the heaviness of earth.
Fly on angel's
Pure wings of love.
Know, the spinning out of universes from within
The shaping of goodness, of kindness,
The crafting of joy for the Friend.
I would serve joy and not bread to my Friend.

"REVEALED"

Come; Lay thy face upon my face.

Put thy hand upon my hand.
Feel; I am fire, worshipped by angels.
My soul, a firehouse.
Happy with the fire.
It is enough to be the furnace,

"LET IT BE"

"Fiat, Jesus, as your mother said it years ago.
Let Spirit overshadow and birth
The Christ in me.
Send your Spirit Breath to
Kindle spark
My body singular-each cell
Vibrating eternal love.
That I might see
With eyes of soul
That I might wonder
At the loveliness of life
And be of good cheer.
I am thy love
Too knowing to punish
Too loving to remember
A healer without medicine.
Boldly
I would speak the Father.
Be threads
Woven into the cloth of God's Holy will.
The raiment of the Most High!"

"GOVERNED BY GRACE"

Long ago I played with Jesus
Washed his face
Hugged his child body
His earthly form
As Mary's handmaiden.
I heard his cries
I answered his calls
I dried his tears.
Now, He hears my cries,
He fashions every cell
Synchronizing each
To the Word's vibration
Once again
I'm Home with Him.

"JAPAN PARK SCENE MEMORY"

Swaying swish of broom stick
Lost in cosmic rhythm's motion
Silence drives this lady sweeping
Free her play in heaven's rapture.
Union realized,
Freedom gained

"LIKE BUTTERFLY"

Creative Caterpillar
Designs cocoon.
I go inside
Make higher room.
Butterfly sheds legs to fly
I loose my lower self for sky.

"Resurrection"

Radiant presence
Shine forth
In this deep darkness
Where stars hide in walnut shells
Enclosed and growing sweet in Spirit
Ten billion forms vibrating Source
Ripening forth
Resurrection
Immortal diamonds shine

"PAIRING UP WITH GOD"

We think of pairing up with God,
On last breath breathed, on leaving Earth.
Church taught, lie bought, Eden lost.
Here's the marriage, Eden's Power.
A love song singing here this hour.
Calling us to court Divine.
We, the harp, we play the love song
With our heart string,
Now,
Eden here on Earth

"IN OCEAN TUNNEL"

Within this tiny house of time
We share this moment.
Together, we breathe the breath within the breath
What greater union?
You and I sharing the Secret One Within
How perfect the choice, this union
No longer surfing single wave
We surf full Ocean Wave
Sheer joy!
No end to the tunnel.

"SACRIFICED"

Who will be sacrificed today?
Jump Up
Be first to answer the cry.
Be altar of adoration
Don't cling to this troubled illusion called "myself".
Beloved calls
Be sacrificed.
Be the grave, make it a rose garden
Where the Presence, the Origin
Will bless you with thousands of rose bushes.
Die before you die
Lest you be the rooster
Eating the single grain of corn in front of him.
And not the field of corn
From which it came.
You're ocean fish
Swim in the Ocean
That feeds itself to its fish.

"I Ask Today"

I ask today
"How are you not today?"
"What have you not seen?"
"What is your form not thirsting?"
The answer reveals the Way.
Don't try to paint on water
That's insubstantial

"Desire"

Passionate
I call to the mountains,
Only echoes return.
You hide.
By grace alone
You come to me.
My night is too long,
Come tryst with me!
In this topsy- turvy world
I am a straw of no worth.
Shh, it's a secret.

I'll choose my soul.
Lest the dragon's fire burns!
Master of myself, free from desire,
Pure and radiant
Priceless Pearl
I wait to see the Face of God.

"GARDEN ASH"

Winter wood waiting to be burned.
Burn!
Be winter daylight
Lest you live as winter night,
Instead of Garden Ash
That Births gold flames of
Sacred Union.

"A Plane Bound for Home"

It is the hour of the heart
Homeward bound.
I serve as stewardess on this plane

I will be fire today melting icy hearts
Bringing blankets that cover faults.
I will serve joy on lunch trays
Pass out water from wishing well
Smile fear away when danger threatens
"All is well! God is Good."
On this plane bound for Home.

"LOVE'S PROTECTING"

Walking through dangerous ravines,
Steep ditches filled with thorns and darkness
Where anxiety would crowd out the heart,
I let the Beloved walk before me to make
Sunset into a sunrise.

He protects, keeps my feet those of a bride
With no trace of bruises, of scratch, of mud.
He, a full moon, lighting up my landscape

"LOVE TRANSFORMS"

Light enters in proportion to the opening of the heart.
Open up my heart, for I thirst for more of You.
Open the top of my head
That I might reach the Heavenly Throne of Love
Let the full rose of the Human Divine
Open in me.
Surrendered wholly to the Light
Make each petal of my being be in full bloom.
Seeing the Beloved in You,
I am transformed into Love itself.
You live in me—the Divine Human Love
You in myself—one single Light.
Gate of Love, throw flames into my heart.
Annihilate me in the presence of Divine Love
I come raw—cook me until I am ash.
God's hidden saint—transformed.

"PLANTED BY WISDOM"

God's Wisdom planted him next to me
That I might see more of this precious Golden Man.
Have I done something good in some life time?
Or has grace filled this moment and blessed me?
Still, my shyness stays, except in poetry,
That he might see me planted next to Him.

"THE FATHER'S WORK"

Searching for my inner nature
I look to him, my fellow traveler
I find the one inside who walks like Jesus
When he walked on water,
The one inside who turns water into wine.
I praise and glorify the Father.

"CHANGE"

I have practiced loving God in darkness
But suddenly I'm loving in Light

"POSSIBLE GRANDEUR"

I am the candle,
With light tearing against the wick,
Allowing brilliant radiance by
Escaping into the Fire

"THE FRIEND"

Imparting wisdom by his lovingness,
My friend leads me to the threshold of Myself.
For alone, I hold a Wisdom and knowledge of God.
Yet in his silence, my heart ceases not to listen to his heart.
In his absence, what I love most in him is clearer,
As from the plain, the mountain is clearer to a climber.
The purpose of our friendship?
The deepening of the Spirit-the expansion of life.
The Spirit dwells in rhythmic silence
In the truth of his loving heart.
I keep it as the taste of wine remembered.
That God be done in us.

"LOVERS WITHIN"

How have we not lived today?
Our eyes see geese flying above.
Have we seen the Beloved's expression in them?
Have we seen who's courting us in flying geese?
Our taste delights in sour, salty, bitter, sweet.
Have we tasted Bounty in them?
Or, have we dined this banquet alone?
Our ears hear patter of raindrops, sound of thunder.
Have we heard Love's call in them?
Have we spoken a return message?
Our nose smells baked bread, jasmine fragrance.
Have we smelled the deeper Fragrance?
Or, have we pinched nostrils to the Essential Oil?
Our beings get cradled in hugs and kisses.
Have we touched the true Lover?
Have we understood Beloved's hiding?
If not, how little we have lived,
Living on the outside, not living from within.
"Wake up!" Love's living us.
Have we wakened to this Love today?
How have we not lived this day?

"WE ARE ONE"

A single star,
Sheltered in a shimmering sky
Spoke to the sea.
"I see me in you."

The calm, clean, clear Sea replied.
"You see because there is Silence in me.
It's clarity, the seeing, the knowing."

Wisely the knowing star spoke,
"Your Hydrogen, Oxygen,
Came from me.
You are a Star Child."

Then the ocean lovingly spoke from its place of knowing,
"We're One."

"BE FREE"

Don't look to be richer
Don't keep score
Don't be afraid of losing
Don't have interest in personality
Don't fear what may happen.
Be too full to speak.
Be one who is looking out from within.
Be without walls so there's no need for the latch.
Be the faithful lover.
Be wildly open to express the secret image tightly held within.
Stay in the company of lovers.
Beg to give away your life.
Open your hands to the universe,
Give away each instant,
Free.

"TRUST YOUR LOVE"

Trust your love. It is making a heaven.
Ego's doubt s, disappointment, rejections-
Illusions making a hell.
There is not a thee, me, we
There is only "One"
Be free.

"Hu -Love Force"

Spring's fresh, green leaves, so is love tender.
Fresh French pastries, so is love delicious.
Faithful polestar, so is love steadfast.
Basketball's clean shot from the Zone,
So is love from within.
Hurt forgotten, so is love kind.
Unbendable iron, so is love strong.
Brilliant, faceted diamond, so is love illuminating.
Simple violet placed among radiant roses, lavish lilies,
So is love, ordinary.
Lotus blossom opening slowly, so is love patient.
"Hu," God's Love Force expressing

"HIDDEN SAINT"

I've met one of God's hidden saints.
Will I ever be the same? No!

My thirst for God never quenched before,
Now, expanded.
He has opened up my heart to want more of God
Ready for greater revelations.

In him, I know the eternal Beloved.
We radiate one single light.
Surrendered wholly to the Light,
Let the full rose of the human divine open to us,
Be like stars that vanish into the light
Of the Sun of Reality.

"Hidden Within"

Pregnant bushes, looking baron of leaves,
Wait quietly to bring forth life.
Maturing within, a rose garden of love,
Designed to express the Holy of Holies.

Be not the impatient gardener on the path
Filled with hurried expectations.
That's death or deformity to the forms.
Simply remember what is hidden within,
Bow, bend low.

"LOST IN LONGING"

Longing for the wrist of the King,
A falcon lost, far from home,
I ask, "When is the wedding night?"

The imposter hides the Presence
A trickster, for I know
The King is here.

The angels sing:
"Know thyself
Within thy heart
The Throne"

"BELONGING TO THE KING"

My mind is in fragments
Like bits of wax,
Scattered over many matters.

I must scrape them together
So the royal stamp can be pressed into Me.
I belong to the King.

"On Dying"

When I leave this world,
Don't say I have passed,
I have died,
Tell the truth.
I was dead.
I came to life.
I ran off with the Beloved.

"MILK OF LOVING"

I shall be like the child
Cry out my pain.
A mother, I know the wanting cry
That makes mother milk flow.

I renounce the path to disease, death,
Renounce the stolid and silent in me.

Weeping is a great recourse.
I cry out loud
Let the milk of Loving flow into me.
This day, I choose to be Child.

"DRAWING GOD NEAR"

Bringing joy to a single heart,
Better than building a thousand shrines.
Enslaving one soul with love,
Better than setting free a thousand captives.
If people want to draw God near,
Seek Him in the hearts of others.

Printed in the United States
By Bookmasters